DON'T CRY,

DON'T BEG

LYNNETTE C. ANDERSON

TABLE OF CONTENTS

INTRODUCTION

O ne salient feature of humans is the fact that we are emotional beings. We have varying emotions that cause us to act and react in different ways. A lot of times, these emotions are pivotal because they affect the way we live our lives and also affect the way we interact with other people.

Although it is normal for all humans to feel these emotions, it is, however, important to understand these emotions. In understanding these emotions, you will need to take out time to personally understand yourself. A lot of times, these emotions are personal, and that is why we need to pay attention to them.

In this book, we will take a look at one of the most misunderstood emotions that we feel as humans- anger. One common misconception about anger is the fact that most people claim that it is unhealthy. Well, anger is a very healthy emotion, and it only becomes unhealthy when it is not controlled.

If you have ever met someone with chronic anger issues, you would wonder why such a person reacts that way. At the end of this book, you will have gotten a proper introduction to anger management. I will also teach you several practical tips that can be used to deal with anger issues and also help you to maintain great relationships with people.

Consequences of Chronic Anger

There are numerous negative effects that explosive anger can have on a person. It affects such a person's health, relationships, as well as, his/her general state of mind. A person with chronic anger issues will often have regrets after certain actions that often happen at the spur of the moment.

Anger becomes chronic when you are unable to think before taking further action in a tensed situation. As one of my childhood mentors used to tell me,

"If you cannot control your anger then you will be easily controlled by people". When people discover a weakness in controlling one's anger, they tend to take advantage of this to the fullest. A person who fails to control his/her anger will often lose control during several situations. However, the good news is that getting your anger under control is not as difficult as you think it is. Self-evaluation is important because it helps you to slow down during those moments when you would ordinarily act irrationally.

Can I Totally Stop Getting Angry?

Unfortunately, anger cannot be totally crushed because it is simply a way of passing across a message. Anger simply tells you that the situation that you are in is upsetting or threatening to your person. The problem arises when you cannot control yourself during times like these.

Anger cannot be crushed, however, it can be controlled and we will highlight the vital ways through which anger can be controlled.

This way, your reaction to situations around you will become more thoughtful. This is great because it helps you to understand the message that is contained in the emotion as opposed to explosive reaction whenever you feel the emotion.

Anger only becomes a problem when its expression leads to harm on yourself or others around you. I have come across people who have the most appalling misconceptions about anger. One of these misconceptions is that it is healthy to vent your anger in certain situations. Some people even go as far as commending a show of anger as being a show of power through which one can express their displeasure with an event or a person.

People with anger issues often try to justify their anger through various mundane interpretations. However, as a professional in the field, I have discovered that a hot temper is never the way out. As a matter of fact, it often makes matters worse than it originally was.

Think of it, most of the wars that started since the world began are due to man's inability to curtail anger. A lot of times, we tend to believe that reacting in a detrimental way sends a strong message to the people around you. When things get out of hand and the "beast" in you is unveiled, it is necessary to tame that beast.

Over time, I have noticed people perceive it as easier to vent and be hot-tempered, than not. However, real strength exists when you are able to stay in control of your emotions. When you are able to control your reaction to this emotion then you will live a better life. In this book, I will give you practical steps with which you can understand the anger and handle it effectively.

If you know anyone that feels like it is out of their hands and they have accepted being referred to as being temperamental, know there are better ways through which emotions can be expressed, and we will take a look at these ways in subsequent chapters of this book.

Another common misconception when it comes to anger management is that it is meant to help you suppress your anger. However, this is far from the truth; the goal is not to ensure that you do not get angry anymore. Personally, I think it is impossible to let go of anger. I mean, there are countless examples of ways through which people will get on your nerves. You could be driving on your lane in traffic, and a reckless driver dents your vehicle.

What do you do when a situation like this arises?

This is a great question that we must understand. Are you supposed to come out of your car feeling happy that someone just hit your vehicle? Of course not! It is never a healthy goal to subdue your anger. Rather, the goal is to ensure that you understand the message behind the emotion. At that moment, it is best that you evaluate a range of options and eventually go for the one that would yield the most favorable result.

When you understand the message behind the emotion, then you will find it easier to deal with it effectively. This simply means that you can deal with your anger without losing control. When this happens, it often leads to regrettable actions which often have dastardly consequences.

On the other hand, when you are able to actively control your anger then your life will get better. You can get your needs met at all times, and you will also find it easy to manage conflicts. A good number of problematic relationships suffer simply because of the lack of control. When you understand the emotion and subsequently master the right reaction to it, then you will find it easier to manage your relationships.

Relationships get stronger when you master the art of managing conflicts (of interest).

Rome Was Not Built In a Day

The journey to the mastery of an emotion such as anger is not a short one. It takes time and commitment to ensure that you get it. With anger management, you will need to put in constant practice to ensure that you master it. The great thing about managing your anger is that it gets easier by the day.

No matter how bad you think your anger issues may be, there is always a way out. There are times when professional help needs to be sought, however, that in itself is not as stressful as many people assume. You simply need to be willing to let go of the baggage that comes with being temperamental.

Why Did I Write This Book?

This is one question that I always love to ask myself whenever I am writing a book. I have come across several books that talk about anger management and all that has to do with it. I have also read numerous articles (both online and offline) about the importance of anger management. However, most of them come from the perspective of avoidance or accepting people's wrongs and dealing with it.

This project is focused on individuals who seem to be verbally aggressive. A lot of times, we fail to see the aggression in people's words and often think that anger is only manifested through physical actions. This book is made for you whether you occasionally get out of control or you have had times when you (moderately) caused physical harm as a result of your anger. This book is also produced for anyone who is terrified of their anger. I understand what anger looks like, the regret, the nerves, the deep breathing, the flight or fight response, and many more.

If you find yourself constantly harboring intense feelings of anger, hostility, and resentment towards others, then this book is meant for you. This does not mean that you are any worse than the persons who do not harbor these feelings; what it simply means is that you need some understanding.

Also, if you are someone who might have committed acts of physical aggression towards others as a result of your anger, then this book is also for you. A lot of times, we are quick to reprimand people for being too hot-tempered. The truth is that most people that feel this way do not necessarily like it. However, there are certain attributes that many people subconsciously get used to as they go through life. Often times, it gets to the

point where they wrongly assume that these kinds of responses are natural to them.

There is never a point where anyone is irredeemable. If you pay attention to people who have intense anger issues, you will find out that these outbursts often happen as a result of certain stressors. This is not a way of excusing such behavior; however, these stressors often lead to actions that are not well-thought out.

Also, when anger is not properly understood and subsequently managed it may lead to overactive hostility (even at the slightest and most insignificant irritants). When this happens regularly, it creates a tag with which people address you. As a human being, it only takes a matter of time before you consistently assume that it is your nature to act that way. This kind of nature is also characterized by swift and harsh judgments that often lead to regrets.

Recognizing Anger Issues

Anger issues often arise as a result of an individual's inability to control the outcome of their anger. Remember that I said anger is not such a terrible emotion? However, the reaction of an individual is what truly matters.

Have you ever caught yourself saying things that you would ordinarily not say as a result of anger? It is a pattern that sticks if you fail to pay attention to it. It starts with swift judgment and subsequently leads to your body language. Signs such as glaring looks, a clenched fist or jaw, are just a couple of factors that you notice when this pattern begins.

At a later stage, this may lead to passive-aggressive patterns such as social withdrawal. At this point, it gets increasingly difficult for the individual to follow simple direction and rules. That individual often gets provoked by authority even when it is meant to be in his/her favor.

When this happens, such an individual finds themselves frequently challenging authority. This subsequently leads to the show of disregard and disrespect for those in positions of power. Often times, it has nothing to do with the person or the position that such a person holds; it is simply a result of uncontrolled anger.

Another sign that manifests in folks who have no control over their anger is the use of abusive language. If you find yourself always using harsh words (even at the slightest provocation), then you may need to pay attention to your response to emotions. People that use abusive language do that in a bid to intimidate other people and assert some sort of 'power.'

The thing about excessive anger is that most people know that they suffer from it. As a matter of fact, they are often aware that their reaction to anger

often has negative consequences; however, most people falsely assume that they cannot help it.

Effects of Anger

Another common misunderstanding when it comes to anger issues is that people use substances as a means of coping. Various substances such as drugs and alcohol are used as a means of keeping calm. This is never a good option (even if it manages to calm you at that point). Dependence on these things may likely lead to further complications in your health. Therefore, it is best to stay away from them. Later in the book, we will look at healthy ways to deal with anger.

There are several reasons why anger is considered bad; it is an emotion that may cause negative consequences when it isn't properly handled. When anger gets out of control it, it may lead to several negative consequences.

To conclude the introductory part of this book, let's take a look at some consequences of uncontrolled anger:

It has negative effects on your physical health

Anger, when it is not controlled, can take a toll on your physical health. This is because it causes you to operate at high levels of stress. When the body consistently goes through stress it causes aging, amongst other things. Uncontrolled anger may also cause individuals to become more susceptible to certain conditions as a result of a weakened immune system.

It has negative effects on your mental health

Consistent bouts of uncontrolled anger will eventually lead to the depletion of your mental energy. When this happens, it has several negative effects on your brain. Uncontrolled anger can cloud your thinking and cause you to be less productive. This may eventually lead to an increase in workload, coupled with, subsequent stress which is also bad for your mental health.

It negatively affects the way you relate with others

When anger is not controlled, it may cause you to take things out of proportion as a result of an emotional reaction. When this happens, you tend to see every spec of difference as a problem. A lot of times, our differences help us to get better, for me, I have found it healthy to learn from constructive criticism. However, if I were someone with uncontrolled anger, I may frequently take offense at such gestures.

I hope this introduction has shed some light on the subject matter. The goal is to ensure that you totally understand what anger is and subsequently discover how to effectively deal with it so that it doesn't have negative effects on your life.

CHAPTER 1

EXPLORING ANGER

The goal of this chapter is to explore anger and all that is behind it. This part of the book is supposed the truths about anger. I have had several people send me messages about certain perceptions that they might have heard at one point or another. This chapter will be dedicated to answering all your queries and affirming those that are true.

Before we go ahead, let me make it clear that anger is often a cover for other feelings. Anger may occur as a result of trauma from an awful experience in the past; however, it is more commonly associated with stress. These factors can make an individual more susceptible to a lack of control over anger.

Most times, we lack control over anger because we fail to understand the feeling. Other times, anger occurs as a result of fear, hurt, shame, insecurity, and many more similar feelings. The reason why you got angry and snapped after someone said something to you is not anger. Upon closer review, you may realize that the person touched on an issue that you are insecure about. It is best that you ensure that you understand your emotions and can tell one from another. This recognition will help you to effectively deal with the situation.

In most cases, anger is used to mask people's actual feelings. People who grew up feeling like it is not right to express yourself may end up using anger to mask their true feelings. As humans, it is crucial that you express yourself adequately. When you are able to do this, then you will know yourself and this knowledge will help you get better.

When you can recognize your strengths, then it becomes easy to also identify your weaknesses and work on them. When you fail to recognize the weaknesses, they become subsequent manifestations of uncontrolled anger. The lack of control that occurs during anger may also be as a result of underlying health issues such as consistent stress and depression.

To effectively deal with uncontrolled anger, you need to ensure that you reconnect with your emotions. This way, you will accurately point out what the problem is and deal with it instead of venting wrongly.

Recognizing (Uncontrolled) Anger

Like I said earlier, anger often manifests as a result of certain emotions that can be expressed and handled in the right manner. Therefore, it may be difficult to differentiate between these emotions and anger. While it is okay to express these other emotions, it is not okay to lose control and express them as anger.

There are certain traits that can help you to recognize that your anger has gone beyond the norm. I'd outline these traits and call them the characteristics of anger. Let's take a look at some unique factors that can help you to discover that your anger is getting out of hand.

When Anger Does Not Allow For The Expression Of Other Emotions

A lot of people tend to misunderstand the true meaning of being strong. There are folks that believe that the manifestation of anger is pretty healthy. As a matter of fact, some cultures have attributed the emotion to strength and hailed people who got angry as a way of "showing" strength and precision. However, this is a misconception that is very far from the truth. It is common to see people replace emotions such as fear or guilt with anger to avoid seeming weak. Real strength lies in the proper awareness of your emotions and the proper channeling and expression of these emotions. When you find it hard to express other emotions apart from anger, then there is a problem. Emotions are outlets that can be used to express how you feel about various events or circumstances around you. When you fail to recognize and apply these other emotions, you may find it difficult to control your anger.

Anger Does Not Compromise

A lot of times, anger arises from an individual's failure to recognize other people's point of view. When you find it difficult to concede defeat or accept that you are wrong then you may have anger control issues. A lot of times, people use anger as a way of getting things done the way they want it to happen. This becomes the only option when you are someone who is scared of failing or being vulnerable. If you find yourself always wanting to have things go your way and you feel terrible when it doesn't then you may need to check yourself. What is the reason for this kind of emotion? Is it because you are a goal-oriented person who puts in so much work and expects the same kind of results or is it simply as a result of ego?

These are the kind of questions that you will need to ask yourself during the process of self-evaluation to properly understand your emotions.

Anger Causes An Individual To Feel Intimidated By Varying Opinions

An individual who finds it hard to see things from other people's point of view will certainly view every opposing opinion as a challenge. If you find yourself feeling intimidated because of the fact that you are wrong, then there is a problem. You need to look inward and find out why you feel this way. It may be due to low self-esteem, and it is a harmful trait because it causes you to make enemies due to the fragility of your ego. It is normal for every person to have a sense of pride and self-respect. However, if it gets to the point where you feel the compulsion to always be in control, then there is a problem.

You need to be open to varying perspectives and ideas to properly control your emotions. The strongest people aren't those that always need to be in control, control is acheived when you can understand people's perspectives and learn from them. It not only helps you to control your emotions, but it also helps you to learn more and build stronger relationships in all areas of your life.

My goal for every reader is to ensure that the overall intensity and frequency of angry outbursts is controlled. This can be done by ensuring that you focus on understanding emotions as what they really are. Anger cannot be avoided, but you can learn to resolve situations without escalation. By doing this, you will eventually find it easy to express your anger in a controlled manner. A lot of people become unreasonable when they get angry. This is very detrimental for those who are around you, and it often projects you as an unreasonable person who cannot relate respectfully with others. Uncontrolled anger causes people to often overlook the good sides of your character because it often brings out the beast in you.

This is why it is primary for you to have an awareness of the things that trigger anger in you. You also need to be aware of the warning signs that remind you that you are in an angry mood. This will help you to ensure control over your anger when it eventually arrives. Remember that I said the process of controlling your anger takes absolute mastery?

You need to pay attention to ensure that you master the warning signs. It is impossible for your body to suddenly explode into anger, it is always a gradual process, and it involves physical, as well as, mental signs.

When you feel these signs, you can prevent yourself from getting angrier. Physical signs may include: quicker breaths, headaches, clenching of your hand and jaw, needing to release energy and quicker heartbeat, to mention a few.

When you study yourself and understand the signs that apply when you feel in your "angry mode," it will help in better controlling yourself as the situations arise.

CHAPTER 2

NOTICING THE PATTERNS

A wise man once mentioned that if you can count to five before making a decision, then it is likely that you will make a better decision. Thinking about consequences is enough motivation to manage one's anger effectively. It helps you to calm yourself down before you react negatively as a result of other factors.

People always find excuses for their anger. You hear about "the man in traffic who suddenly changed lanes" or the "woman who was wasting time at the counter." There are several scenarios that can be imagined; however, most (almost all) of them are simply negative patterns that eventually lead to an outburst. When it comes to controlling your anger, your reaction to the situation is what really matters. I hear a lot of people talk about the situation and how impossible it was to not lose control.

Most times, the things that cause your anger are not real. They mostly come as ideas in the mind of the perceiver and these ideas come about as a result of certain reasons. I will take a look at 4 of them:

Jumping to conclusions

Anger outbursts are often caused by conclusions that often jump out without prior consideration. These conclusions are often as a result of the belief that such an individual knows what the other parties involved are thinking. For example, someone mistakenly hits 'X' while running and in return, 'X' decides to run after the person to return the favor. However, unbeknownst to 'X', the person has a vision impairment and didn't see 'X'

There are thousands of similar examples that take place in our daily affairs. We tend to assume the worst and make decisions based on these assumptions. I have been in situations where I could not possibly defend my actions without sounding like a liar. These things happen every now and then and that is why you need to avoid jumping to conclusions.

The Rigidity of the Mind or Perceptions

Have you ever met someone who was convinced that situations are meant to happen in a particular way and anything else is seen as being wrong?

The rigidity of the mind also has to do with having preconceived notions based on past happenings.

For example, let's say you live in the same building as someone with partial blindness and let's imagine that somehow you fail to notice this condition. You also notice that this person often brushes shoulders with you in passing on the stairway. The right thing to do is to respectfully mention it to the person. However, a person with anger issues may believe that the person is bumping them in order to consistently get on his/her nerves.

A lot of times, people have certain ideas in their heads regarding how people *should* act and as soon as their reality does not match this vision then it creates a problem for them. This is why it is crucial to have a flexible mindset about people and things around you. When you do this then you will not find yourself making false generalizations about situations and others that will subsequently affect the way you react.

Overreacting

There are people who seem to always look for situations to show their anger. It seems as though these kinds of people often tend to pile up negative emotions such as resentment. I always advise people to let their emotions out as soon as they feel it. Harboring negative emotions often leads to a casual buildup that eventually causes you to overreact over the slightest things.

People that overreact over the negatives often find it easy to overlook the positive. They tend to focus on the things that aren't working and mostly ignore those that are.

Casting the Blame on Others

Another common characteristic that is particular with folks that cannot control the outcome of their anger is that they tend to blame everyone and everything for their actions. They often attribute their outburst to external forces without realizing that they are in the driver's seat of their actions.

In order to get rid of toxic responses when you get angry you need to own up to your action. By taking responsibility for your life, you will find yourself making informed decisions as a result.

In order to gain total control of yourself when you are angry, you need to ensure that you take control of your environment. Since you know the things that cause you to react in certain ways then it is important that you avoid the negatives and focus on the positive.

When you understand the effects that stressful events have on your health, you can ensure that you stay away from these kinds of events in order to ensure your own mental safety. Try as much as possible to stay away from people, places, as well as, situations that could bring out the worst in you. This is a crucial step that needs to be taken in order to actively control your environment and the things that you allow in your mind.

Controlling your environment is not a total solution but it helps. If you can learn to control yourself, as well as, your environment then you will be on your way to mastering total self-control during moments of anger. This way, you are less likely to make rash decisions that you may eventually regret.

When enough attention is paid to your routine then you will identify the various activities, people, places, events, and other factors that cause you to be uneasy. For example, if you tend to feel uneasy during traffic, you may decide to listen to your favorite podcasts in traffic. By doing this, you are able to avoid the problems that are associated with being in traffic. Alternatively, you can choose to avoid going out during times when there is heavy traffic.

CHAPTER 3

DEALING WITH ANTISOCIAL BEHAVIOR

There are several ways to describe the term "anti-social" and it often relates to actions that are against the norm in society. Anti-social behavior often has to do with the consistent breaking of rules, lying, stealing, forms of physical aggression and many more.

One common characteristic that is pertinent to anti-social behavior is the fact that it causes frequent confrontation. This happens as a result of an individual's difficulty to subscribe to the general rules that guide the peaceful co-existence of the society.

Antisocial behavior also causes individuals to interact in a confrontational manner. Most times, these kinds of people often try to deliver a message by being argumentative or aggressive.

Another salient factor when it comes to antisocial behavior is the fact that it causes such an individual to lose their sense of humanity. It causes individuals to feel little or no remorse at all when they cause pain to others. People with antisocial behavior also have little or no regard for the truth. They simply find it easier to tell everybody whatever, in their minds, people need to hear.

Furthermore, antisocial behavior also causes individuals to frequently get into verbal or physical altercations. This happens as a result of the four reasons that I mentioned in the last section. People that have antisocial behaviors often try to make up for their shortcomings by seeking special excitement and fun. There is also a pattern of sexual promiscuity and the difficulty to stay committed in relationships because they are not interested in taking on responsibilities.

People with a known history of antisocial behavior also tend to act mostly based on impulse. This happens as a result of instability in their lives which is caused by their inability to commit to personal responsibilities.

How to Deal With It

With these negative attributes, you may wonder if there is any redemption for individuals with antisocial behavioral patterns. The answer is YES! In this chapter, we will take a look at some ways to deal with antisocial behavior in both yourself, as well as, others around you.

The first step when it comes to dealing with antisocial behavior is to take responsibility. A lot of times, people are too ashamed of their actions so they simply decide to continue in that light. They often use violence and force to get through daily activities. However, by simply learning to accept the responsibility for your actions, you are on a path to redemption.

When you understand that you are in charge of your behavior then you will subsequently act accordingly. People who display antisocial behaviors often blame other factors for their actions. In order to deal with it effectively, you will need to keep your behavior within the acceptable societal standards.

Although this is not as easy as it seems. When you consciously demonstrate a healthy sense of respect for social norms then you will find yourself on the right side of things. In order to do away with antisocial behavior, individuals also need to be conscious of the rights of others. This consciousness gradually causes a significant improvement in the manner that such individuals relate to the world.

Most antisocial individuals often tend to have issues with authority because they have problems with organized rules and structures. However, when such individuals become more socially sensitive then they will find it easy to co-exist peacefully with others. In order to stop being antisocial, individuals also need to come to an understanding that they need to abide by prevailing social limits and boundaries. This is important because it helps set boundaries on the actions of every individual and subsequently makes society more peaceful.

In dealing with antisocial behavior, it is important that you recognize and admit the existence of the problem in the first place. The truth is that many people go around with antisocial behaviors and they often fail to recognize it, some simply refer to it as their "nature".

Also, you need to pay attention to the patterns of unethical behavior in order to review and subsequently reduce the frequency of such actions. This may take a while; however, it requires consistent effort. Another crucial point when it comes to dealing with antisocial behavior is trust. People that show signs of antisocial behavior simply need to recognize that trust is the basis for all kinds of relationship. This realization gradually causes the person to have a change of heart especially when such a person learns that it is also possible for him/her to be treated with kindness.

Now, let us take a look at some tips that can be helpful for someone who is dealing with antisocial behavior. They include:

- Making the individual understand the fact that lawfulness is the reason why there isn't anarchy in society. Hence, he/she should ensure to subscribe to the laws in order to forestall anarchy.

- The individual must be willing to make a commitment to live within the rules of society. This is a gradual process that takes time and commitment but it often yields amazing results.

- A person who constantly displays signs of antisocial behavior needs to be made to see the negative consequences of his/her action.

- It is also important to make such an individual see the importance of being sensitive to the needs of others.

- Teaching the individual the importance of reliability and honesty. Most individuals with a history of antisocial behavior often fail to see the benefits of positive traits such as these.

- It is also important to explore the fears of the individual. Most people that act in unacceptable ways often do so as a result of certain fears they have. This is why it is important to explore one's fears when it comes to trusting others and being trusted.

- Lastly, it is important to practice the process of trusting another person as it is an important step when it comes to dealing with antisocial behavior. This last step needs to be demonstrated by learning to trust the people that they care about.

Cognitive Behavioral Therapy

Cognitive behavioral therapy (CBT) is a form of therapy that helps individuals to change negative thought patterns into positive ones. The process of doing this is quite complicated; however, it is a great way to deal with stress, grief, uncontrolled anger, as well as, a myriad of other life challenges.

As humans, the way we think and interpret life's events is pivotal in affecting our behavior. With CBT, an individual can utilize a goal-oriented approach to gain control over anger. It is a form of psychotherapy that is focused on determining how a person's thoughts, beliefs, as well as attitudes, affects the way a person feels. Subsequently, this may affect the behavior of such a person.

Negative thinking patterns are often subconsciously picked up from childhood. Most times, these thoughts are caused by dysfunctional assumptions that are fueled by certain interactions. A lot of times, these negative patterns become habitual for the unsuspecting victim. The foundational idea behind CBT is the fact that human thoughts and perceptions ultimately influence behavior. This means that certain factors in your mind may cause you to have a distorted view of reality.

CBT proves beyond any iota of doubt that people's thoughts can lead to psychological problems. This is why it is important to embrace positive and helpful thoughts in order to gain total control of your mind. With CBT, individuals form new habits in a bid to get rid of existing physical and/or mental conditions. It has been known to help people to deal with challenges such as stress, which eventually leads to uncontrolled anger when it isn't properly managed.

The method was invented in the 60s by Aaron Beck and has been consistently developed since then. Over time, various coping strategies have been formed to help people deal with various kinds of challenges when it comes to mental health.

With the use of CBT, various individuals have been able to gain clarity about several mental issues. It has also helped many to develop a systematic thought process that helps to challenge misconceptions. With CBT, persons can learn to change their perceptions and subsequently better themselves through adequate understanding.

Cognitive behavioral therapy can be used for people of all ages and it is a combination of basic theories of behaviorism and cognition.

CHAPTER 4

PAYING ATTENTION TO THOUGHTS

I find it interesting that the average human is said to have about 70,000 thoughts daily. This is a tremendously high number and it shows the importance of being in total control of your thoughts (and subsequent actions). Most times, thoughts often pop up in our heads almost without your permission.

Consciousness and the ability to reflect on the past and project the future are both amazing features that set man aside from other creations. Consciousness is a great gift because, through our consciousness, we are able to control our thoughts and subsequently control our lives as a result. Therefore, thoughts can be man's best friend or his worst enemy (depending on how well it is used).

What is inside your mind is very important because it often controls the external world and your experience on it as a human being. Your perception of the world is a clear reflection of the activities that go on in your mind. This means that in order for you to see positive changes in your life, you need to correct your thoughts.

If you always have thoughts about fear, hate, or judgmental feelings then it may become the reality that you face. The truth of the matter is that the world remains the same; however, the manner in which you view the world is really important as it determines most of the actions that you eventually take in your life.

Thoughts, feelings, as well as, people's attitude towards the world is a significant factor that controls people's actions. As a matter of fact, the way we interpret events that happen to us and those around us is often a result of thoughts and feelings. I have conducted tests and taught several lessons about the importance of thoughts. These lessons often help people to see how thoughts can actually influence their patterns of actions. Positive, as well as, negative action patterns often occur as a result of the thoughts that precede any behaviors.

In order for change to occur, it is important to recognize the three steps needed for cognitive self-change to occur:

- The first step requires a person to pay attention to their thoughts and feelings. This step is done in order to understand how those thoughts are helping or hurting the individual. The process of self-evaluation is important and you need to patiently go through this process in order to get great results.

- After you pay attention to your thought process, the next step is to ensure that you are able to recognize the potential risks in your thought process. What are the downsides or advantages of thinking and feeling the way you do? By considering this, you will be able to ascertain whether your thought process has been helpful in helping you become a better person. If you discover troubling thoughts and feelings then you need to figure out how to make amends.

- The last step when it comes to cognitive change is the application of what you have been able to discover in steps 1 and 2. The third step requires that you reduce the risks of having a negative life by cutting down on negative thoughts. It is not enough to cut down negative thoughts; you need to replace these negative thoughts with positive ones. Once you are able to do this then you will find it easy to use positive methods of thinking and feeling to reduce the risk of living a negative life. This will give you a positive attitude that will subsequently lead to positive actions.

Thinking Reports

This is another concept that can be used to objectively observe thoughts in a bid to make amends where it is necessary. One golden rule for thinking reports is objectivity, it is crucial that you structure this report objectively in order to get the best out of it. Thinking reports can happen as often as you wish for them too. It serves as a way of accessing the kind of thoughts that control your mind and eventually control your body.

Every action that you perform as a human being was once a mere thought. The process of thoughts becoming action is crucial in the mind-body relation and it is the mind that always communicates what the body should do. There are four crucial parts when it comes to structuring objective thinking reports.

- The first step in the report is the brief description of the situation that is being assessed. Remember that objectivity is pivotal for the success of this process.

- The next step is to make a list of the thoughts that occupy your mind. This is important because it helps you to realize the things that your mind is focused on.

- Subsequently, a similar list of feelings is compiled. This will help in realizing how these thoughts are processed and the subsequent effect that they have on the mind of the thinker.

- Lastly, we will also evaluate the list of attitudes or beliefs that occurred as a result of the thoughts and feelings that were harbored.

The next step after the thinking reports is the process of evaluation. In this process, you get to figure out the kind of thinking that may lead you to trouble. This is known as "risk thinking" and it involves both high risk and low-risk thoughts. High-risk thoughts are those thoughts that are very likely to put you in trouble when they occur. On the other hand, low-risk thoughts often produce a minimal risk of getting you into trouble. You need to pay attention to both kinds of thought because they ultimately dictate the quality of your life.

It is important that you know feelings can be expressed properly when individuals master objective self-observation skills. It is not something that is mastered in a rush; it takes time and consistent effort to gain mastery of one's feelings. When you are able to gain mastery of your feelings then you will find it easier to pay attention to the feelings of other people and respond accordingly.

I said these things to tell you that empathy is very important when it comes to anger management. It is important for you to understand the way you feel and subsequently relay it to the way other people feel and your response to their feelings. This is a crucial social skill that can be used to understand and analyze how people feel in daily interactions.

This understanding makes it possible for an individual to understand and show empathy towards self, along with, other people involved. If you wish to develop positive relationships with people then you need to learn how to respond or react to people's feelings. A lot of people show their insensitivity when it comes to their relationship with others. This often leads to the buildup of negative emotions and in order to avoid this, you need to ensure that you learn to consider other people's feelings.

Introduction to Problem Solving

A lot of people resort to anger as a result of their inability to solve simple problems that they may encounter. This part of the book will equip readers with the crucial knowledge that is needed in order to get rid of old ways of thinking and acting. We will take a look at the 6 steps involved in problem-solving.

Stop And Think

The "fight or flight" response in humans can be used effectively when individuals pay attention to their thoughts, feelings and physical reaction. Whenever you are in a problematic situation (where you may be tempted to overreact) it is important that you stop and think. By paying attention to thoughts and feelings, folks can gain a better understanding of the warning signs when they see them. There are three important steps that individuals can use to effectively stop and a think:

- By being quiet

- By calming down and

- By getting some space.

This process is highly important because it helps in the control of anger. This kind of control is missed by those who react emotionally to things that happen to them. The stop and think technique can be used for spontaneous problems, as well as, problems that afford individuals hours to think it through. Whatever the case may be, when you pause and think about it, you are bound to get solutions that are well thought-out, positive and productive.

Describing The Problem

For the success of this step, individuals learn to contain the problem due to their awareness of the warning signs. This step is also characterized by the objective description of the problem in order to ensure that an efficient solution can be sought. This step is pivotal because it creates what I call an "objective distance" between the individual and the problem that they face. Subsequently, this prevents such individuals from jumping to untrue conclusions.

Gathering Relevant Information

This step is important because it helps the individual in question to consider certain information which helps them to gain clarity. In this step, the individual considers the objective facts, the thoughts and feelings of others, as well as, their own personal opinions and beliefs. This step is pivotal because it considers crucial information with which an eventual goal is set. This step helps the individual to create a goal for what they want out of the situation (as opposed to an emotional outburst).

Evaluate Choices And Consequences

In this step, the individual is required to think about as many possible options with which the problem can be solved. This is great because it helps the individual in question to think of several alternative ways of solving problems. After taking time to consider options, the individual in question is also made to consider the consequences of each of these choices.

Choose, Plan, And Execute

After the process of carefully evaluating choices, the individual then chooses the best possible option from the pool of available choices. After this choice has been made, the individual needs to make a plan on how to go about the chosen option. Lastly, the choice is executed without any hassles.

Evaluate

The process of evaluation helps the individual to accurately determine the choice(s) that hold the best potential for the achieving of their set goal. Remember that the primary goal is to avoid the conflict cycle. Once this choice has been made, the next step involves rolling out an action plan. After the plan has been implemented, the individual finally reviews the solution to ensure that the right choice was made.

CHAPTER 5

ANGER MANAGEMENT TIPS

T he goal of anger management is to ensure that your feelings are expressed in a healthy way. When you do this, then you will have great control over your anger, and you will use it to make positive change. Anger can only be used constructively when you learn to pinpoint the exact things that you are angry about. When you learn to do this regularly then you will master the art of properly resolving issues.

It is important that you figure out the exact thing that you are angry about and why you are angry about it. This will give you clarity and help you to discover the real reasons behind your anger. When you are able to do this, it becomes easier to find a resolution through constructive action.

There are times when you may notice that your anger is beginning to spiral out of control. During times like these, it is important that you take a timeout to cool down. This is crucial because it helps you to take time off to really think about the situation and then figure out what your best reaction is will be.

It is also important to recognize that anger is temporary. This realization is important because it helps you to fight fair while expressing your concerns. Respect is important and necessary no matter what the situation may be. This is why it is important for you to ensure that you do not lose respect for people as a result of anger. Apart from respecting the person, you also need to ensure that you respect the opinions of the other person. As I said earlier, anger is momentary and it is never enough reason to lose vital relationships.

A lot of times, uncontrolled anger happens as a result of focusing on the past. In order to gain control of the situation, you need to focus on the present moment and ensure that you totally understand what is at stake. Conflicts can be really tiring and often times it could have you worn out. This is yet another reason why it is important that you avoid conflicts as a result of uncontrolled anger.

Forgiveness is a critical part of anger management. You need to be willing to forgive yourself, as well as, other people to stay happy. Grudges often cause you to harbor negative emotions that tend to get worse after further provocation. When individuals refuse to forgive, it causes matters to get worse and reduces the quality of one's life.

Differences are always bound to occur amongst humans. However, the way an individual responds to these differences is critical. We have looked at several conflict resolution skills in this book; therefore, you should not get involved in rifts that get you nowhere. It is best to recognize when to disengage and just move on for the sake of your sanity. This kind of decision arises as a result of proper self-awareness that can further strengthen your relationships and your life in general.

Now, let us take a look at some tips that can help individuals to properly manage anger.

- Learn to express your anger in a non-confrontational manner. Ensure that you are calm while expressing your anger. This expression should be done with a goal in mind and it simply involves stating your concerns and your needs. While doing this, it is important that you consider the feelings of the other parties involved.

- Do not speak in the heat of the moment. As a matter of fact, take out time to consider the things you want to say during times of anger. An African proverb asserts that "Words are powerful, once spoken, they cannot be taken back". Ensure that you think before you speak and not the other way around.

- Physical activity such as exercise (and if you cannot exercise try ripping up paper), can help you to significantly reduce stress and subsequently manage anger effectively without hurting other people who are involved. If you feel the signs that inform you that your anger is escalating then you need to refocus your energy on physical activitiy. Not only are these activities pretty enjoyable, but they are also a great way to keep you in check.

- Do not hesitate to take a timeout every now and then. This is important because it helps you to remain calm and avoid stress.

- While it is important to find out your triggers (the things that get you angry) it is equally important that you work on finding solutions to the issues at hand. Anger does not fix anything when you do not attempt to find possible solutions.

- Humor has been known to serve as a great way of releasing tension and lightening up.

- There are several relaxation skills with which you can calm your nerves and think of possible solutions to the problem. Activities such as deep breathing, yoga, listening to music, and many more can be soothing. Relaxation helps you get rid of stress which is known to be one of the main causes of uncontrolled anger.

- Also, it is important that you understand that there are times when you need to seek professional help. If you seem to consistently fail at trying to control your anger then you may need to talk to an expert and ask for guidance. Knowing when you should seek professional help is very important when it comes to anger management.

CONCLUSION

L ife is beautiful and it is meant to be lived to the fullest. This is why it is important to master your emotions so it can help you to better understand yourself and your capabilities. Many times, we tend to react to events or the actions of other people without really considering the grand scheme of things.

No one suffers from the pain of uncontrolled anger like you. This is why it is important that you do not let people get into your head so much that you lose yourself. A lot of times, we try so hard to defend outbursts as being a perfectly normal response for events that happen to us. However, it is better to take the time to understand yourself, your surroundings and your reactions in various situations.

Humans are really powerful beings; our subconscious mind is the seat of most of our thoughts, memories, habits, feelings, and so on. The entirety of your life largely depends on the kind of control that you are able to exert over your subconscious mind. It is important to know yourself properly because this will help you to understand your triggers and subsequently learn ways through which you can respond better to them.

To understand the importance of controlling your anger, you need to look at the downsides of anger as it relates to your physical and mental health. If you are feeling tensed and you are tempted to react in a harsh way, it may be best for you to take consistent deep and slow breaths. This helps you to get fresh air into your lungs, which signals your body to relax.

When do you seek professional help?

Although I have consistently written about how you can help yourself to overcome anger issues, it is not always the case. There are individuals who fail at trying to get rid of anger issues with the use of these methods. When you notice that these methods do not seem to be working for you, then you may need to seek the help of a professional. Individuals may seek the advice and expertise of a professional when anger consistently gets them in trouble with the law or with the people around them.

It is never a bad idea to seek professional help. Although there are people who see it as a sign of weakness, it is the greatest show of strength and the will to become better.

Over the last 20 years, I have worked with several great individuals through the process of CBT and other forms of anger management. These people have seen tremendous results without the use of any kinds of medication. These solutions are easy to learn and based on in-depth research, coupled with, practical application.

I have found out that anger often results from fear. Therefore, if you can effectively deal with fear, then you will find it easy to deal with other emotions including anger.

When you are able to find the root of anger, then you can subsequently find out how you can channel your energy toward more positive things. The great thing about seeking the help of a professional is that the programs are designed to be done at your own pace. This means that there is no pressure and that you can practice and get better on your own terms.

To wrap things up, I will like you to consider a few things:

- At the age 90:

- Do you want to have more memories than regrets?

- Do you want to smile and look back at the great experiences and people that you met along the way?

- Do you want to have people around you who love and care for you?

The truth is that we all want these things. Often times, we tend to look for complex solutions to the simplest problems that we face as humans. When in reality, the solution to most of our problems is simple and straight forward.

It goes beyond anger management or the need to be seen as a sane person. When you understand your emotions and other factors that affect them, then you will be on a path to a lifelong experience of freedom, love, trust, happiness, and many other positive feelings.

Chronic anger is a pretty dangerous emotion and we cannot afford to leave it unchecked. This is because although it may seem like it's not a big deal; it leads to further complications such as aggression and depression. The truth is that no one wants to seem like a monster and this is why it is crucial to effectively manage anger.

It sucks to see people suffer from the shame that comes with the lack of proper anger management. It is my wish to see people break free from the shame, guilt and loneliness that occur as a result of this. It is important that you consider those that you love and care about; gaining control is not difficult when you have the proper tools and the right understanding.

At the start of this book, I had a goal in mind, a goal that is constantly inspired by my love for humanity; a goal that is inspired by the need to see fewer people become victims of negative thinking and sabotaging self-talk. This goal is aimed at helping as many people as possible to overcome the crippling effects of displaced anger. With anger management, you can learn to express anger in positive, productive and healthy ways. Not only will this improve the quality of your mental health, but it will also help you to create and nurture amazing relationships as you advance through life.

My personal belief is:

Every person, regardless of circumstances, can do better, live productively, with the ability to manage their own lives; then teach future generations to do the same.

If you need professional help contact me through my website at www.DontCryAndDontBeg.com

www.ingramcontent.com/pod-product-compliance
Lightning Source LLC
Chambersburg PA
CBHW060558100426
42742CB00013B/2603